Busy Bees

Music and lyrics by
Norma L. Gentner
Illustrations by Joe Veno

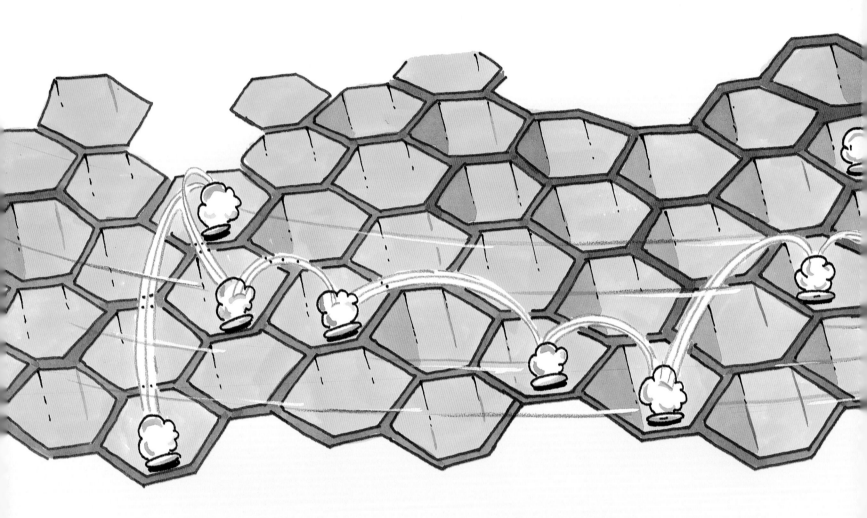

I'm a honey of a honey of a bee,
busy bzz-bzz busy bee.

I'm the queen of all the hive,
laying eggs from nine to five.
Without me, where would bees be?

3

Busy buzz-buzz buzzin'
all through the day—
there is so much work,
I can't ever play.

Just a-buzzin'
and a-hummin' along.
Buzz-buzz!

I'm a honey of a honey of a bee,
busy bzz-bzz busy bee.

I'm the drone
and special mate
when the queen
goes on a date.
Without me,
where would bees be?

**Busy buzz-buzz buzzin'
all through the day—
there is so much work,
I can't ever play.**

Just a-buzzin' and a-hummin' along.
Buzz-buzz!

I'm a honey of a honey of a bee,
busy bzz-bzz busy bee.

I'm the worker who makes honey,
but I don't get any money.
Without me, where would bees be?

Busy buzz-buzz buzzin'
all through the day—
there is so much work,
I can't ever play.

Just a-buzzin' and a-hummin' along.
Buzz-buzz!

We're a group of bees
you call a colony,
busy bzz-bzz busy bees.

When there's work
that must be done,
we cooperate as one.

Fruit and flowers couldn't be without bees. Buzz-buzz!